Avi's

The True Confessions of Charlotte Doyle

Study Guide

BookCaps™ Study Guide
www.bookcaps.com

Table of Contents

Disclaimer

This study guide is an unofficial companion and not endorsed by the author or publisher of the book.

Historical Context

Edward Irving Wortis was born on December 23, 1963 in New York City; he received the nickname "Avi" from his twin sister Emily. Avi grew up around literature and creativity in his younger years as his grandfathers were both authors, and one grandmother was a playwright. Avi recalls his mother reading to him and his sister when they were young and often bringing them to the library. Avi attended a private school in New York City where he was tutored by a woman named Ella Ratner, whom Avi gives credit for the success of his writing career, as she encouraged him to continue writing despite suffering from a writing disorder called dysgraphia. Throughout his extensive writing career, Avi has penned more than 70 novels spanning multiple genres and age groups, though he mostly gears his writing toward adolescents and young adults. One of Avi's most well-known and celebrated novels is *The True Confessions of Charlotte Doyle* (1991) which tells the story of a wealthy thirteen year old girl who finds herself traveling from England to the United States alone on a ship called Seahawk. *Charlotte Doyle* earned Avi many awards, including the Newbery Medal in 1991, as well as a Newbery Honor. As of 2012, *The True Confessions of Charlotte Doyle* is being adapted into a screenplay.

Plot

Charlotte Doyle is a young girl from high society who is traveling from Liverpool, England to Providence, Rhode Island to meet with the rest of her family. There is supposed to be another family aboard the ship that will look over Charlotte while she is aboard, but she learns that there will be no one to accompany her. Charlotte is to travel aboard the *Seahawk* and is confused when porters and crewmen seem fearful of its leader, Captain Jaggery. Once aboard the ship, Charlotte immediately takes a liking to Captain Jaggery, whom she sees as a true gentleman. When a black sailor called Zachariah tries to befriend her, Charlotte thinks he is kind but also inferior to her and believes she should not associate with him. Jaggery asks Charlotte to spy on the crew for him, and when she learns of a mutiny they are planning, she immediately tells the Captain.

After exposing the mutiny, Charlotte learns what kind of evil man Captain Jaggery actually is, and she begins to fall in with the crew. Charlotte becomes a crew member herself and embraces the liberation that she feels for the first time in her life. Captain Jaggery makes many attempts to bring Charlotte down, but she excels at every task he gives her. During a storm one night, a crew member winds up dead and Jaggery accuses young Charlotte of the murder; the crew says nothing because they believe one of their own to be guilty and want to protect him. When Charlotte is sentenced to death, the truth finally comes out that Jaggery is, in fact, that responsible party and Charlotte works with Zachariah to take him down. Back in Providence, Charlotte no longer finds joy in her upper class lifestyle and runs off to join the crew on the *Seahawk*.

Themes

Identity

When Charlotte first boards the *Seahawk* she has always been a young girl from a privileged background. She often questions her own identity and makes the reader question who she is, as well. Zachariah makes a comment that if Charlotte's father is anything like her then he will help take down Jaggery, but Charlotte realizes that she is nothing like her father. Charlotte often compares herself to others, at first as though she is on a pedestal and at the end as though her family no longer understands who she is.

Gender

Charlotte certainly stretches typical gender roles during her time aboard the *Seahawk*, which prompts both Captain Jaggery and her father to refer to her as "unnatural". While Charlotte starts out as a prim and proper young lady, she soon finds she is happiest wearing sailor clothes and doing manual labor with the crew; she even cuts her hair short and develops calluses on her hands. While Charlotte is obviously female, she regrets being seen as dainty and fragile and prefers to be seen as a force and an asset.

Transformation

Charlotte truly comes into her own throughout the course of the novel. At the beginning, she knows only her life in the upper echelon of society, but she is curious about the things she is not familiar with. She learns that just because a person presents themselves well does not mean they are good. Charlotte realizes that the person she wants to be is one who is tough and capable, who fights for what they believe in, and who is loyal to those who are truly worthy of trust. By the end, Charlotte realizes that the world she belongs in is much different from the one she is living in.

Order

Captain Jaggery is obsessed with order and with everything being in a specific place, literally and figuratively. His cabin is highly organized, and he prefers for his crew to be organized and to never fall out of line. The consequences for a person going against Jaggery's plan of order are devastating, and the captain is unscrupulous in his punishments. It is not until Charlotte notices that Jaggery's fine furniture has been damaged by the storm and hears him mumbling about order that she realizes the lack of order has truly driven him out of his mind.

Justice vs. Injustice

There is always a dichotomy between these two concepts aboard the ship. When justice is served for one group of people, injustice is served for another. When Jaggery beats Zachariah nearly to death justice is served for him, but the rest of the crew feels it is unjust. Similarly, Charlotte is found guilty of a murder she does not commit which feels just for Jaggery because he blames her for destroying his order but for Charlotte it is truly an injustice. Finally, when Jaggery falls into the sea, justice is achieved for the crew who believe he had it coming, though for Jaggery, it would have certainly been seen as an injustice.

Education

Charlotte is well-educated, and at the beginning of her story she believes that her education makes her better than those who are not educated; this idea undoubtedly comes from her father who seriously values education and a high social standing. Charlotte immediately judges the crewmembers for being less educated than her, or for not knowing how to read. As Charlotte gets to know the crew and falls in with them it becomes obvious that she no longer judges them on their education but rather on their strength of character. Education becomes learning skills rather than learning subjects for Charlotte, and she finds that skills are more useful than what she learns in books.

Class Systems

There is a distinct line between classes in the world that Charlotte comes from. Her family is well-off and high society. As a part of this world, Charlotte is taught that she is better than those beneath her, especially servants or crew; this is why Charlotte immediately was drawn to Captain Jaggery and tried to brush off Zachariah. Once Charlotte got to know the crew members and realized the reality of Captain Jaggery she learned that a person's money, power, stature, or status means nothing if they are not honorable, trustworthy, hardworking.

Freedom of Choice

Charlotte leans to exercise her freedom of choice during her time on the *Seahawk*. As Charlotte comes from a place where she is not given much choice in her life (as evidenced by Mr. Grummage's refusal to listen to her at the beginning of the story), once she comes into her own she truly takes life into her own hands. Charlotte begins to make big moves; she chooses to become a crewmember, to cut her hair, to take down Jaggery, and to leave home to be a sailor for good. The more choices Charlotte makes for herself the more liberated she becomes.

Bravery

It is ironic that despite the fact that Charlotte is the youngest person aboard the ship and a female she is also the bravest. Jaggery acts tough but is terrified of the order and fear he has instilled on his crew being shaken in any way. The crewmembers act as though they are strong men but when time comes to stand up for themselves against Jaggery they cower in his presence. Charlotte is the character who stays true to what she believes and has no fear in the face of the Captain, or death.

Acceptance

Despite living a sheltered existence, Charlotte begins to accept the crewmembers before they begin to accept her. She makes choices which align her with the crew in the hopes of gaining their trust, support, and guidance and their trust and acceptance of her comes slowly afterward as she did snitch on them initially when she learned of their impending mutiny. By the end of the story not only have Charlotte and the sailors fully accepted one another but Charlotte has also learned to accept herself for who she truly is.

Characters

Charlotte Doyle

Charlotte Doyle is the narrator of the story. She is a head-strong young girl from a family of high society embarking on a two-month voyage from England to Rhode Island on a ship lead by the tyrannical Captain Jaggery. Charlotte learns quickly that it is not a person's social standing that matters but who they are inside, and she soon abandons her roots to live the life of a sailor. Charlotte is fearless, brave, sassy, and loyal despite the hardships she faces aboard the *Seahawk*. By the end of the story, Charlotte has truly learned who she is and what is important to her.

Captain Jaggery

Captain Jaggery is the captain of the *Seahawk*. Charlotte takes an initial liking to Jaggery because he has the appearance of a true gentleman, but she soon realizes he is anything but. Jaggery is obsessed with order; he does everything based on a strict schedule, he keeps his crew in line with a strong arm, and he is highly organized. To preserve order Jaggery is abusive, merciless, and downright cruel to the men aboard his ship; when Charlotte turns on him he treats her even worse than his crew. Eventually, Jaggery's need to have everything in order becomes his downfall because the rebellion against him drives him insane.

Zachariah

Zachariah is the oldest crewmember aboard the *Seahawk* (around fifty years old), and he is also the only black man; he believes he and Charlotte are a lot alike because they are so different from everyone else. Zachariah acts as a doctor, cook, and general handyman aboard the ship. He immediately befriends Charlotte though she is initially put off because she believes she is better than him. Zachariah proves to be a terrific friend and ally to Charlotte and helps her to form a plan which will eventually bring down Captain Jaggery.

Mr. Hollybrass

Mr. Hollybrass is Captain Jaggery's first mate aboard the *Seahawk*. Mr. Hollybrass is commissioned to do all of Captain Jaggery's bidding, such as stringing Zachariah up and whipping him. During the hurricane Mr. Hollybrass is found with Charlotte's knife sticking out of his back, and she is immediately blamed for his murder, as he was also holding her handkerchief in his hand. Later Zachariah informs her that he saw Jaggery and Hollybrass arguing that night. When confronted Jaggery admits to the murder but thinks Charlotte should still pay.

Mr. Keetch

Mr. Keetch is Captain Jaggery's second mate aboard the *Seahawk*. Charlotte feels strange around Mr. Keetch because she finds him to be perpetually nervous and skittish. When Zachariah and Charlotte are planning to rise against Jaggery after he has sentenced Charlotte to death they bring Keetch into the loop, not realizing that Keetch had actually been working as Jaggery's spy the entire time he has been aboard.

Mr. Cranick

Mr. Cranick was a crewmember aboard the *Seahawk* on the previous journey to the one Charlotte joins. Mr. Cranick had gone against Jaggery, and as punishment he was beaten until he lost his arm. Much to Jaggery's surprise Mr. Cranick appears when the crew stages a mutiny on their current voyage. After Mr. Cranick speaks up against the Captain, Jaggery wastes no time fatally shooting him in the chest. At Jaggery's insistence, Cranick's body is simply thrown overboard rather than being given a proper burial.

Barlow

Barlow is one of the crewmembers on the *Seahawk*. When Charlotte first arrives at port to board the ship, Barlow is one of the first people who tells her she should turn around and get on a different ship. Barlow is the crewmember who is responsible for getting Charlotte to the brig when she is accused of the murder of Mr. Hollybrass and he says nothing to Charlotte until she asks him whether he believes she did it; he simply tells her he does not know and leaves her alone.

Fisk

Fisk is another of the crew aboard the *Seahawk*. He is one of the more outspoken members of the crew, though, like the others, he is fearful of Captain Jaggery and his cruel punishments. After Jaggery believes that Zachariah is dead Fisk is told to take over Zachariah's job as cook. Later on, when Charlotte sees the ad in the paper for the *Seahawk*, it is revealed that Fisk has been named as the new captain of the ship after the death of Captain Jaggery.

Ewing

Ewing is one of the crewmembers that Charlotte first becomes close with. When she is reading to him one day while he sews, Ewing breaks a needle and Charlotte goes off to find him a new one; this is when Charlotte learns of the first mutiny. Ewing loves to talk about his girlfriend back in Scotland. He is one of the friendliest men aboard the *Seahawk* and tries to keep a lighthearted atmosphere despite the wrath of Jaggery.

Mr. Grummage

Mr. Grummage is a man who works for Mr. Doyle. It is the job of Mr. Grummage to get Charlotte safely aboard the *Seahawk* and unite her with the family who is to watch after her on the journey. Despite obvious clues that Charlotte should not board Jaggery's ship Mr. Grummage insists that she take it anyway, as her father wants her on it. Even when Mr. Grummage discovers that Charlotte will be the only female aboard the ship he still insists and even seems quite annoyed with suggestions otherwise.

Mr. and Mrs. Doyle

Mr. and Mrs. Doyle are the upper-class parents of Charlotte, Albert, and Evelina. Charlotte compares all men to her father at the beginning of the novel as she sees him as the epitome of a gentleman. Mr. Doyle is a businessman who is quite successful and who places a high priority on education. Despite the fact that Mr. Doyle provided Charlotte with her journal he does not believe the story she wrote in it and burns it, criticizing her grammar. Charlotte decides her father is too like Captain Jaggery, and she does not want to be a part of his lifestyle anymore. Charlotte's mother is a typical upper-class woman and is horrified by Charlotte's appearance and behavior when she gets to Rhode Island.

Grimes

Grimes is another member of the *Seahawk* crew. Grimes is supportive of Charlotte's efforts to become a crewmember and to learn the tricks of the trade. It is Grimes who teaches Charlotte to use a knife when learning to cut ropes and sails. When Charlotte is accused of murdering Mr. Hollybrass, it is Grimes who admits to Captain Jaggery that he is the one who taught her to use a knife, though he is not necessarily admitting that he thinks she is guilty.

Mr. Johnson

Mr. Johnson plays a small role in the novel, but one of importance as he is the only member of the *Seahawk* crew who does not sign the Round Robin signifying mutiny against Captain Jaggery. Because of his loyalty to the Captain, he is promoted to second mate, which demotes Mr. Keetch.

Albert and Evelina Doyle

Albert and Evelina are the younger brother and sister of Charlotte Doyle. When Charlotte arrives in Rhode Island Albert, and Evelina do not try to hide their disgust at Charlotte's filthy appearance, or her shortened hair. Albert and Evelina are much the same as Charlotte was when she first boarded the *Seahawk,* and she notices the clear difference between herself and them when they are reunited. Mr. Doyle refuses to allow Charlotte to tell Albert and Evelina about her journey.

Bridget and Mary

Bridget and Mary are servants of the Doyle family. When Charlotte arrives in Rhode Island, she dislikes that Bridget and Mary always refer to her as "Miss" and is disappointed when they refuse to call her by her first name, for fear of what her father would say. Though Bridget and Mary are supposed to keep watch of Charlotte because of her questionable new behavior, Charlotte convinces Bridget to sneak her a newspaper. Charlotte uses the paper to find out when the *Seahawk* is setting out again.

Chapter Summaries

Chapter One

It is June, 1832 and Charlotte Doyle is preparing to board a ship from England to America where she will meet up with her parents. Mr. Grummage, a businessman who works with Charlotte's father, has accompanied her to the shipyard and is responsible for getting her aboard safely. Charlotte marvels in the "delicious chaos" that surrounds her. The ship that Charlotte is to sail on is called the *Seahawk* and is manned by Captain Jaggery. The porter who is carrying Charlotte's trunk immediately gets a strange look on his face at the mention of Jaggery's name and drops the trunk without a word. Both Charlotte and Mr. Grummage are confused by the man's actions so they flag down another porter and pay him, though once they reach the *Seahawk* the porter drops the trunk leaves just as the first man.

Mr. Grummage gets on the ship to find the families which will be looking after Charlotte on her trip, and while he does Charlotte takes in all of the details of the massive vessel. Mr. Grummage returns to Charlotte and she can tell that he is troubled. At first Mr. Grummage does not tell Charlotte what is wrong though he eventually reveals that the families who were supposed to accompany Charlotte will not make it so she will be sailing alone. Charlotte is concerned being the only girl on a ship full of men but Mr. Grummage insists that she will be fine and must follow the orders of her father.

Chapter Two

Mr. Grummage accompanies Charlotte onto the boat
where they meet the second mate, Mr. Keetch. Mr.
Keetch is the one who is in charge of the ship while
Jaggery and his first mate are on shore, and he
advises Charlotte to take another ship to America. At
this point Mr. Grummage has heard enough and
leaves, insisting that Charlotte must remain on the
ship. Charlotte is taken to her room by Mr. Keetch
and she is appalled by the conditions she will be
traveling in; there is little furniture and it is quite
shabby. A man called Barlow brings Charlotte her
trunk and once again tries to urge her to depart from
the ship; he speaks on behalf of the other sailors.
Charlotte does not believe a man of Barlow's position
has any right to speak to her that way, and she sends
him off. Once Charlotte is alone in her room, she
allows herself to have a good cry because she is
scared and alone.

There is another knock on the door and Charlotte answers it to find a black man named Zachariah. Zachariah is a bit of a jack of all trades, and he is also the only sailor aboard the ship who is black. Charlotte notes that he looks terrible, but he has a sweet voice. Zachariah asks Charlotte if she would like to have some tea and Charlotte is comforted by this suggestion because it reminds her of being home, and also of being around more civilized people. Zachariah thinks that he and Charlotte have a lot in common and should stick together; she is the youngest as he is the oldest, and she is the only female as he is the only black person. Charlotte thinks that this suggestion is far out of line as she does not need Zachariah for a friend. Before he leaves, Zachariah gives Charlotte a small knife to use for protection though she does not want to take it at first. That night as Charlotte falls asleep with the knife under her mattress she hears Mr. Keetch and someone else talking about her in the hall saying "they" will not move as long as Charlotte Doyle is aboard.

Chapter Three

When Charlotte wakes she has decided that she is going to get off the ship, however, when he walks out on deck, she finds that they are already out to sea. Charlotte sees Mr. Hollybrass, the first mate, ring the bell and all of the sailors including the captain appear on deck. Charlotte is impressed by Captain Jaggery as he looks like a distinguished gentleman, unlike the other men aboard the ship. Mr. Hollybrass takes roll call of all the sailors, and they all appear to be there; he also tells Captain Jaggery that he could not get them to "sign the articles" though Charlotte does not understand what that means. Jaggery asks about a Mr. Cranick but Mr. Hollybrass is not familiar with the name, nor does he appear to be aboard the ship. Captain Jaggery speaks to the crew, telling them that they will obey his every order as he is the leader of the ship and what he says goes. He tells them that they must work hard, and he gives them extra rum and sends them off. Captain Jaggery introduces himself to Charlotte and seems to be polite, however, when she asks to be let off the ship he tells her that it is not possible. He asks her to have tea with him and promises to protect her while she is aboard. When Charlotte gets back to her own cabin, she gets dizzy and becomes ill. While she is sick, Zachariah takes care of her and the Captain visits a few times. In her sick haze, Charlotte recalls throwing her knife at a rat she sees eating her journal.

Chapter Four

In the morning, Charlotte finds the knife on the floor
and decides to give it back to Zachariah. On the
deck, Charlotte runs into one of the sailors,
Dillingham, who disappears when he notices that
knife she is holding. Finally Charlotte finds
Zachariah in the gallery where she tries to give him
back the knife, but he will not take it. Instead,
Zachariah offers Charlotte some more tea and a hard
lump of bread that the sailors eat called hard tack.
Charlotte learns from Zachariah that she had been
asleep for four whole days, so she should eat. When
Charlotte agrees to eat, Zachariah tells her the story of
why she needs to keep the knife. He tells her that the
crew is planning a rebellion against Captain Jaggery
because he is a tyrant; he beat the man called Mr.
Cranick to the point that he lost one of his arms.
Charlotte is skeptical of the story because she found
Captain Jaggery to be a gentleman, but she does recall
hearing the name Mr. Cranick so she does not know
what to think. Charlotte learns that the men aboard
the ship are the same sailors that worked with Jaggery
last time because no one else is willing to; this
reminds Charlotte of the men who refused to carry
her luggage aboard the *Seahawk*. Zachariah tells
Charlotte that all of the sailors are aware that Jaggery
works for Charlotte's father. Mr. Hollybrass comes
into the gallery and asks Charlotte to have tea with
Captain Jaggery in his quarters.

Chapter Five

Charlotte decides that she believes nothing of what
Zachariah has told her and she is appalled that
someone as lowly as him would speak to a person of
her pedigree in such a way. Once again Charlotte is
highly impressed by Captain Jaggery; his quarters are
beautiful and stylish and he is dressed in fine clothing
while reading the Bible. Captain Jaggery welcomes
Charlotte and shows her a photo of his daughter
Victoria who is five. Jaggery encourages Charlotte to
preach to the sailors aboard the ship and to teach them
morals. Charlotte thinks that the Captain is a lot like
her father, and she tells him so; she thinks that she
could easily be friends with this man. Jaggery tells
Charlotte that he often has to treat the sailors in a way
that may seem cruel, but he does it because it is the
only way to assert his dominance and maintain order
on the ship. Captain Jaggery wants Charlotte to keep
an eye out for any suspicious behavior amongst the
crew, and he shows her a mysterious picture of a
round-robin to look out for. Charlotte decides that
she trust Jaggery enough to show him the knife that
Zachariah gave her though she says it is from Mr.
Grummage because she feels that she should not
reveal that it came from Zachariah. Charlotte is
willing to give the knife to Jaggery, but he tells her
that she should keep it in case she needs to protect
herself.

Chapter Six

When tea is over Captain Jaggery releases Charlotte
to Mr. Hollybrass. As she is leaving, Captain Jaggery
kisses her on the hand in front of the entire crew, and
Charlotte is beside herself with his gentlemanly ways.
Mr. Hollybrass takes Charlotte to meet Mr. Barton,
the man who will take her to find her trunk, which has
been placed in the ship's cargo. When Mr. Barton
brings Charlotte into the cargo hold he leaves her to
herself for a little while to go through her things in
peace, but Charlotte does not feel as though she is
alone; she feels like someone is watching her. In the
flickering candlelight, Charlotte looks around to see
if anyone is in the shadows, but she does not see
anything at first. Then when Charlotte looks toward
the ladder she sees a face staring back at her and
smiling. Suddenly the candle goes out, and Charlotte
is immersed in darkness.

Chapter Seven

In the darkness, Charlotte reaches for the knife which she is thankfully carrying on her. She speaks into the darkness asking if anyone is there with her but hears nothing in response. As she moves toward the face that she saw, she realizes that it is simply a face that has been carved out of a large nut. Charlotte is shaken and starts up the ladder but realizes she never got the items she came for. Charlotte grabs the clothing and books she wanted out of her trunk and climbs back up the ladder, happy to leave the cargo hold behind her. Charlotte wonders if maybe Mr. Barlow planted the head with the intent of scaring her, but then she thinks he may be too passive for such a move. Charlotte thinks that maybe she did see two different faces when she was down there in the darkness, and the first one just might have been human. Charlotte prefers not to think of such things, so she decides that the candle must have been blown out by a draft in the small space and the head that she saw was actually just the carved face the whole time. Charlotte thinks that she is crazy for getting so scared at a carving, so she decides she will not tell Captain Jaggery because she does not want him to think she is some silly child. Charlotte thinks that the Captain and Zachariah seem to be fighting for her friendship, and she wonders why that might be. She thinks that she should continue to be kind to both, but her allegiance should lie with Jaggery. Charlotte puts the knife back under her mattress where it belongs.

Chapter Eight

Charlotte starts to settle into life on the ship. Every morning she prepares herself to meet Captain Jaggery on the deck, but she is dismayed that all of her dresses have become filthy from being aboard; she decides to set one dress aside so she will look nice for her arrival in Providence. Zachariah brings Charlotte her breakfast each morning which consists of hard bread, molasses, and terrible coffee. At lunch, Charlotte is subjected to the same undesirable meal and then at dinner she is given a small amount of meat with rice and beans with the same terrible coffee as the other two meals. Each Sunday the men bathe, shave, and put on clean clothes then Charlotte reads to them from the Bible as she told Captain Jaggery she would. Every day Charlotte meets with the Captain for tea and tells him what she has observed around the ship; this is the highlight of her days.

Charlotte spends a lot of time with the men aboard the ship, and she enjoys their stories about adventure and fantasy; she also thinks that spending time with her is good for the men. The men grow used to Charlotte quickly and even become fond of her. Charlotte spends time with Zachariah and laments that he is the butt of jokes at times, though the sailors do appreciate Zachariah's knack for cooking. Charlotte has gotten to know Zachariah; he is 50 though he looks older, he is illiterate, and he does not know anything about the teachings of the Bible. Charlotte is offended by Zachariah when he gives her a set of clothing that looks like crew clothing, but back in her cabin she tries it on anyway. Charlotte notices how hard Jaggery pushes the crew, especially when the ship comes to a standstill in the middle of the ocean. Charlotte tries to tell Jaggery he is too hard on the crew, but he does not listen. She knows that a storm is brewing, but it is coming from the crew not from the sky.

Chapter Nine

Charlotte is hanging out with one of the
crewmembers called Ewing one day on deck, reading
to him. As Ewing is patching up an old jacket, his
needle breaks and Charlotte quickly offers to go to
the crew quarters to get him another from his box.
When Charlotte reaches the door to the forecastle
(where the crew stays) she hears the men inside
having a conversation about "putting down marks";
they also suspect Charlotte of spying on them for the
Captain. When Charlotte enters the room she notices
that there are three men relaxing in the hammocks
and Fisk, who opened the door to let Charlotte in.
She looks in Ewing's chest and finds the needle she is
looking for but also finds a pistol; she recalls Captain
Jaggery telling her that the only guns aboard the ship
are in his own quarters.

On her way out of the room Charlotte is flustered and trips over a chest which causes several papers to fall; she notices that one of the papers has a Round Robin on it which is the symbol that Jaggery told her to look out for. As soon as Charlotte leaves the room, pretending that all is well, she decides to tell Captain Jaggery what she has seen. Charlotte runs into Mr. Keetch on her way back to Ewing but she does not think he suspects anything of her. Charlotte realizes that she has seen more people than she should have; there should only be four men who are not on duty at the moment and she recalls four people in the forecastle as well as Ewing. She wonders who the fourth man in the forecastle could have been; a stowaway perhaps? On Charlotte's way to see Captain Jaggery, she runs into Morgan, and she can feel Foley staring her down. Charlotte is nervous about going against the crew but continues to the captain's quarters where she tells him and Mr. Hollybrass what is happening. Jaggery wants the crew called to deck immediately so he can put an end to the mutiny before it begins.

Chapter Ten

Captain Jaggery and Mr. Hollybrass prepare themselves for battle with a large arsenal of weaponry from the Captain's personal stash. When the duo heads to the deck to confront the mutinous crewmembers Charlotte is instructed to join them, though she is not exactly pleased about it. On deck, the crew is armed for a fight, and they are clearly excited to confront Captain Jaggery. Charlotte notices the extra man from earlier and she sees that he has no arm; she realizes this is Mr. Cranick, the man she had heard about from their previous trip. Captain Jaggery also notices Mr. Cranick in the group of crewmembers and confronts him. Mr. Cranick holds up the Round Robin and tells Jaggery that he is not fit to be the Captain and should step down. Captain Jaggery wastes no time in shooting Mr. Cranick in the chest, killing him. The entire crew is visibly shocked, and they decide to drop their weapons, which Mr. Hollybrass promptly collects from them. Zachariah, the only crew member who was not armed, is asked to throw the body overboard rather than giving it a nice burial, but he refuses. Jaggery next asks Mr. Hollybrass to do it but he does not want to either, though he eventually gives in. Captain Jaggery wants to know who is next in command after Mr. Cranick, but no one will come forward. Jaggery asks Charlotte to choose someone to take the punishment, but she only shakes her head in awe of what she is being asks. Captain Jaggery tells Zachariah to step forward and take responsibility.

Chapter Eleven

When Zachariah is called forward, the Captain asks
him if there is anything he needs to say as the voice of
the entire crew. Zachariah speaks, not on behalf of
the crew but in his own defense. He muscles up the
courage to tell Captain Jaggery what a horrible and
unjust Captain he has been to his crewmembers; he
even tells Jaggery that he is the absolute worst
Captain he has ever worked for. Though Zachariah
was not accepting blame for the crew's mutiny,
Captain Jaggery takes Zachariah's speech as a
confession for arranging the entire thing. Captain
Jaggery menacingly asks the crew if anyone wants to
agree with what Zachariah has said, but they all
remain silent out of fear.

Zachariah is strung up by Mr. Hollybrass to prepare for a whipping. Charlotte wants to leave because she feels sick to her stomach, but Captain Jaggery insists that she stay and watch the punishment unfold. Zachariah is to receive fifty lashes of the whip, but Charlotte cannot stand to witness such injustice; she lunges herself at Mr. Hollybrass and grabs the whip from him. In defense of herself, Charlotte swings the whip around and hits Captain Jaggery right in the face. The Captain yanks the whip from Charlotte's hands and beats Zachariah mercilessly until Charlotte is pretty sure he is dead. Zachariah is taken down by the crewmembers and brought to the forecastle leaving Charlotte on the deck by herself. Charlotte has never felt so alone as she gets sick over the side of the ship.

Chapter Twelve

Back in her cabin Charlotte is in tears over her
involvement in what she just witnessed. She thinks
that Captain Jaggery was harsh in his actions, but she
should apologize to him anyway because she cut his
face with the whip. In the Captain's quarters,
Charlotte makes her apology, but the Captain does
not accept it; he is furious with her for making him
look bad in front of the crew and he refuses to protect
her any longer. When Charlotte returns to the deck
she sees the crewmembers assembled beside a canvas
hammock which she assumes holds Zachariah's body.
The crew holds vigil over the hammock and then
allows it to fall into the sea. Charlotte tells the
crewmembers that she is sorry for her interference,
and Fisk tells her that it is best if she just sticks by
Captain Jaggery. Charlotte tells the men that she
hates the Captain, but they all just stare at her and say
nothing. Charlotte runs back to her cabin where she
allows herself another good cry.

Charlotte soon hears a bell that she knows means everyone needs to be on deck. Charlotte sneaks up to observe what is happening but keeps herself hidden. Captain Jaggery is rearranging the ranks of the crewmembers; Mr. Keetch is now second mate while Mr. Johnson has been promoted to first mate because he is the one person who did not sign the Round Robin. Also, Mr. Keetch is now placed in Zachariah's position. Captain Jaggery expects the crewmembers to take turns working an extra shift to cover for having one less man. Morgan feels that this is unfair, but Jaggery insists that they are in a state of emergency now. Charlotte heads to the galley and finds Fisk who answers her questions about what just happened. Charlotte wants to join the crew and pick up the slack, but Fisk condescendingly tells her she is a lady and a passenger so she will do no such thing. Back in her cabin Charlotte puts on the workman's outfit that Zachariah had given her and returns to deck, insisting that she be put to work.

Chapter Thirteen

Fisk will not agree to Charlotte becoming a crewmember himself, so he tells her to present her case with the rest of the crew and see what they think. It is the consensus of everyone else that if Charlotte can manage to climb to the top of the highest mast, which is approximately 130 feet high, then she can be a part of the crew. Charlotte is unsure how to go about the task so Fisk suggests that she go up one of two ways: either she shimmy up the post or she climb the ratlines like a ladder. Charlotte decides that the ratlines are the way to go. The men are mostly supportive of Charlotte; Barlow wishes her luck and Ewing warns her that she may not want to look up or down while she is climbing. Charlotte slowly but surely sets about her mission and somehow manages to make it all the way to the top, though she is utterly exhausted. On the way down Charlotte loses her footing and begins to fall though she is able to right herself with the help of a rope. When Charlotte is close to the bottom Barlow offers to catch her if she wants to jump, but Charlotte actually wants to make it the whole way down by herself. When she finally reaches the deck the crew cheers for her and she is immensely proud of herself. At that moment, Captain Jaggery makes an appearance on the deck.

Chapter Fourteen

The Captain questions Charlotte's clothing and her intentions. Charlotte tells him that she is a member of the crew now, and she refuses to go back to her cabin when he tells her to. Jaggery tells Charlotte that he will not treat her any differently than the rest of the men and that she will be known as Mister Doyle in the ship's books. The crew is happy to have Charlotte as one of them. Charlotte soon realizes that the Captain was not kidding when he said he would treat her just as the others; she lives in the forecastle, and if anything he was harder on her than the others. Charlotte enjoys being a part of the crew; she has her own hammock with a sail around it for privacy, she begins to curse like the men, and her skin toughens up.

One day on deck some line gets tangled, and Jaggery makes Charlotte climb up and fix it. Charlotte has to ease herself out onto the bowsprit, which is the front of the ship, and cut the line loose, but in the process she falls and finds herself dangling over the water. Charlotte manages to right herself and returns to the deck. Jaggery tells her that the men changed course for her so the waters would be calmer and he does not seem to be happy about it. Charlotte thinks Jaggery a coward, and she tells him so as she spits on the deck next to his feet. The Captain simply turns and leaves though he is clearly displeased. Charlotte notices a blue bird in the water one day and thinks it means they are nearing land, but she is told it means a hurricane is near. Charlotte is terrified when she learns that Captain Jaggery plans to steer them into it with the hopes of using the hurricane winds to speed up the journey.

Chapter Fifteen

Charlotte has been aboard the ship for forty-five days when the hurricane hits. As Captain Jaggery likes to ride Charlotte harder than the rest of the crew he makes her climb up and cut down the foreyard sail to save the mast. Charlotte begins the climb with a knife between her teeth and even cuts off her own hair mid-climb because it kept getting in her way. As Charlotte begins to cut the ropes, she loses her balance and drops her knife. Charlotte is hanging by one hand when a figure swoops in and pulls her back up to safety; Charlotte is sure the figure is Zachariah though when she looks around she does not see him anywhere. The crew begins to clear the deck, and they find Mr. Hollybrass dead with the knife Zachariah gave Charlotte in his back. Captain Jaggery sees pulls something from Mr. Hollybrass' hand and Charlotte recognizes it as her own handkerchief. Jaggery sends the crew below deck with Mr. Hollybrass' body. Charlotte is confused as she helps to man the pumps. Later when the storm is over Charlotte is finally able to sleep.

Chapter Sixteen

After fourteen hours of sleep Charlotte wakes and
heads to the deck where she sees the entire crew.
Charlotte asks whether they had forgotten about her
and she is told that they were asked not to include her.
Charlotte finds it strange that everyone has begun
referring to her as "Miss" again; the men eventually
admit that Captain Jaggery has accused her of
murdering Mr. Hollybrass. The men know that it was
Charlotte's knife and handkerchief found on Mr.
Hollybrass' body and the Captain has stated that she
must have done it to avenge Zachariah. Charlotte
wants to tell the men that she saw Zachariah, but she
does not; she wonders whether she saw a ghost or an
angel but knows it was a miracle whatever it was.
Captain Jaggery formerly accuses Charlotte of
murdering Mr. Hollybrass and tells her that the trial
will be the following day. Barlow is commissioned to
lock Charlotte up in the brig, and he does so in
silence; he only speaks to tell Charlotte that he is
unsure what to believe when she asks whether he
believes she killed Mr. Hollybrass. Charlotte is alone
in the dark thinking about her trial when she hears
footsteps approaching. Charlotte does not know what
to think when she sees Zachariah standing in front of
her.

Chapter Seventeen

It does not take Charlotte long to realize that she is not seeing a ghost; it is truly Zachariah standing before her. Zachariah tells Charlotte that the crew pretended to bury his body at sea to protect him from Captain Jaggery but really he has been hiding out in the cargo hold. Charlotte is astonished that no one told her until Zachariah points out that she had snitched on them for the mutiny. Zachariah did, in fact, help Charlotte during the hurricane, but he disappeared quickly because he did not want the Captain to know he was still alive, and he is sure that his secret is still safe. Zachariah wants to go to the police when they arrive in Rhode Island to turn Captain Jaggery in for his cruelty, but Charlotte thinks that it is unlikely that anyone will take the word of a black sailor over a man like Captain Jaggery. Zachariah hopes that Charlotte's father will help, if he is anything like his daughter, but Charlotte is skeptical.

Charlotte tells Zachariah that she was accused of murdering Mr. Hollybrass, which is a situation that Zachariah has heard nothing about. Charlotte tells him that the crew does not seem to be in support of her; she thinks they believe she did it. When Zachariah goes to get some hardtack and water Charlotte wonders if maybe Zachariah killed Mr. Hollybrass and the crew is protecting him because only he and Captain Jaggery knew where the knife was hidden. Sitting in the dark Zachariah tells Charlotte unsavory stories about the crewmembers, which only makes her further believe he could be responsible for Hollybrass' death. When Charlotte sees a light coming she gets back to the brig quickly. Captain Jaggery has arrived to bring her to the trial.

Chapter Eighteen

A courtroom has been established on deck where
Charlotte will be tried. Captain Jaggery will act as
judge for the trial and the crew will sit as jury and
witnesses, sworn in by the Bible. Charlotte pleads
innocent to the murder and declines when asked if she
would like to withdraw her stance as a crewmember.
As there is no one else that Charlotte wishes to accuse
of Mr. Hollybrass' murder the questioning begins.
Captain Jaggery begins by establishing that Charlotte
is a liar, as she originally told the Captain that Mr.
Grummage had given her the knife rather than
Zachariah. After some questions which are asked
with the intention of making Charlotte look guilty
Captain Jaggery has decided Charlotte is an
"unnatural" sort of girl in that she carries a knife and
joins a ship's crew and, therefore, it is reasonable that
she would commit an "unnatural" crime such as
murder. When Charlotte admits that seeing Zachariah
get beaten to death was upsetting for her, the Captain
decides that is her motive and she is found guilty of
murder. As no one defends Charlotte, she is
sentenced to death by hanging, leaving her confused
and terrified.

Chapter Nineteen

Charlotte is taken back to the brig by the Captain, and when he leaves Zachariah lets her out. Charlotte shares the news of her trial with Zachariah and admits to him that she believes he is guilty of murdering Mr. Hollybrass. She even tells him that the crew thinks he did it too which is why they would not defend her. Zachariah insists that he was not the one to kill Mr. Hollybrass. He admits that Captain Jaggery saw him during the hurricane; Jaggery and Hollybrass had been arguing on deck when Jaggery noticed Zachariah. Zachariah initially believed that Jaggery thought him a ghost because he never went looking for him after that but now realizes that Jaggery did not say anything because he wanted to have leverage in accusing Charlotte of murder. Charlotte and Zachariah now believe that Captain Jaggery must have killed Mr. Hollybrass himself. Zachariah knows that the crew must stage another mutiny, but they must steal the Captain's weaponry to do so. Luckily, Charlotte knows exactly where the key is hidden.

Chapter Twenty

Charlotte informs Zachariah that the key to the safe
where the guns are held is behind the picture of
Jaggery's daughter in his cabin. Zachariah leaves
Charlotte alone to find a crewmember so they can
form a plan. While Zachariah is gone, Charlotte
thinks of her family for the first time, and she
wonders whether they would be proud of her when
they find out what she has been doing. Zachariah
returns to Charlotte and he has Mr. Keetch with him.
Keetch is informed that Jaggery killed Mr.
Hollybrass, not Charlotte. Keetch admits that the
entire crew assumed it was Zachariah, and that is why
they stayed quiet; Charlotte was right. Keetch tells
Charlotte that they are close to Providence, and that is
why Captain Jaggery wants the hanging to happen so
soon. The plan is going to be for Keetch to get
Captain Jaggery away from his cabin and for
Charlotte to sneak in and grab the key which she will
pass off to Zachariah. It is one o'clock in the
morning when Keetch sends word that he has pulled
the Captain away, so Charlotte makes her move. She
recalls hearing a conversation behind closed doors on
her first day and vaguely wonders what it was in
regards to. Just then Charlotte enters the Captain's
quarters and finds him sitting there at his table
waiting for her.

Chapter Twenty-One

Captain Jaggery tells Charlotte that he has been waiting for her; it turns out that Keetch is the one Charlotte had heard on that first night, and he had been acting as Jaggery's spy since the beginning. Jaggery tells Charlotte that she disrupted the order and he admits to the murder though believes that Charlotte should take responsibility because she is "unnatural". Charlotte thinks there is a good chance that Captain Jaggery is losing his mind. The Captain gives Charlotte three choices on what she can do next: she can have the gun keys and stage a mutiny which will shame her family, she can go back to being a girl and beg the Captain to forgive her, or she can suck it up and be hanged. Charlotte refuses all three options and runs from the cabin to the deck.

On deck Zachariah has been tied up by Keetch and all the crew is standing around him. Captain Jaggery yells to the crewmembers that Charlotte tried to murder him, and they all stand in silence, even when she yells back that it was Jaggery who murdered Mr. Hollybrass. Captain Jaggery fires his gun at Charlotte and barely misses as the ship pitches. Charlotte shimmies out onto the bowsprit and the Captain follows her, though he is not as agile as Charlotte and loses his balance. As the ship pitches once more, Jaggery falls into the sea. Grimes hands a knife over to Charlotte, and she uses it to cut Zachariah free of his restraints. Zachariah suggests to the crew that Charlotte become the new captain as it was she who finally took down Jaggery.

Chapter Twenty-Two

Charlotte's name is written in the books as captain of
the ship though Zachariah does the actual work.
Charlotte is sad when it comes time for her to go
home to her family because she has changed so much
during the two months she has been aboard the
Seahawk. Charlotte is happy to see her family, but
they are disgusted with her appearance and make
many comments about it. Charlotte's father reminds
her that he wants to read her journal when they get
home. Back at the house, Charlotte shows her family
her now shortened hair, and they are appalled; she
tells them she got lice and had to cut it off which only
disgusts them further. During dinner, Charlotte
accidentally mentions that she conversed with the
crew of the ship, and everyone is aghast at this news.
Charlotte's father tells her she may leave the table as
he thinks that she needs to get some sleep.

Charlotte tries to get the maids, Bridget and Mary, to call her by her first name, but they insist on referring to her as "Miss" for fear of her father. Mary has been given the job of destroying Charlotte's clothing, and when Charlotte goes downstairs she finds that her father is destroying her journal. He tells her that her stories are "unnatural" and he is appalled by her spelling. Charlotte is forbidden to talk about her time at sea and spends a lot of time in her room. She convinced Bridget to bring her newspapers, and one day finds just what she is looking for: an advertisement for the *Seahawk* which will leave port again soon. When Charlotte is finally trusted to be on better behavior she is let out of her room. Later that night, she goes to the docks where she meets with Zachariah and tells him that she is ready to come home.

About BookCaps

We all need refreshers every now and then. Whether you are a student trying to cram for that big final, or someone just trying to understand a book more, BookCaps can help. We are a small, but growing company, and are adding titles every month.

Visit www.bookcaps.com to see more of our books, or contact us with any questions.

42621575R00033

Made in the USA
Lexington, KY
18 June 2019